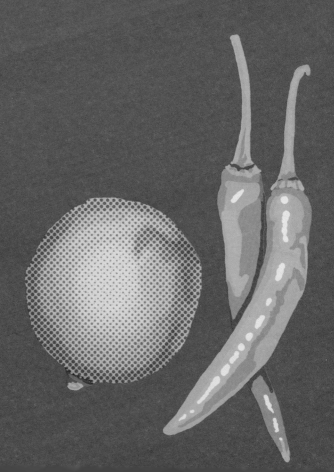

ALSO IN THE BLASTA BOOKS SERIES

blastabooks.com

AGAK-AGAK

Written by Sham Hanifa

Illustrated by Nicky Hooper

CONTENTS

INTRODUCTION

Agak-agak (pronounced aga-aga, with a silent k) is a Malaysian saying that means 'guess-guess' or 'use your instincts'. For me, this simple philosophy sums up the secret of cooking as I experienced it growing up in Taiping, close to the west coast of Malaysia. You can follow a recipe but for the final stages, use your instinct and your palate to judge the levels of spice, salt and sugar. Taste, taste, taste! Does a dish need more salt, less salt? More sugar, less sugar? In this way, a recipe becomes personalised.

My multicultural background is reflected in my cooking. I was born and raised in Malaysia but my father's family is Indian and my mother's family is Thai and Chinese. (Atong is my Thai name and one that was used by family and friends when I was growing up.) These different influences could manifest in our breakfast choice on any given day – it could be a Chinese noodle soup, a traditional Malaysian nasi lemak or an Indian roti canai.

My hometown is Taiping. It's a progressive town and as well as being known for having the most rainfall in Malaysia (so Ireland was no shock for me on that front!), it had a lot of firsts in the country – first train station, first museum, first prison and first zoo, for example.

My childhood home was full of food. It was the hub for big family celebrations like my sister's wedding, when we erected a marquee for 500 people at our home and served them chicken sambal (page 20), rendang (page 34), rice and vegetables.

My late father was a butcher so he contributed the meat to the household. Sometimes he would bring home a takeaway with roti canai or bao, rendang, fish curry or noodles.

But my love of cooking is most definitely because of the influence of my mother, Nang Nian (Nancy), and my grandmother, Nang Boot. My Thai grandmother cooked at the Buddhist temple for the monks and at street food hawker stalls. At home she kept a bountiful kitchen garden at the front and the back of the house, with green chillies, limes, green beans, mango, guava and other fruits and herbs. She lived with us and cooked in the house and my strongest memory is of the smell of green chillies and limes, something that is replicated in my recipes in this book. Her tom yum (page 36) is a strong flavour memory too, with galangal and lime leaves and chilli from her garden.

At the age of 12 I began working part time in a restaurant, trimming and deboning chicken and making broth, fried rice and curries. I worked my way up to more sophisticated Malaysian cultural food before moving on to an Italian restaurant. As an adventurous young man of 20 seeking new experiences, I answered an advertisement in Malaysia and found myself in a taxi from Dublin Airport to a new hotel in Carrick-on-Shannon, County Leitrim, in the west of Ireland at the auspicious turn of the new millennium. That journey would continue onwards, taking me from general kitchen work to becoming a chef at an award-winning restaurant to chef-owner of my own restaurant and café, exposure on Irish television and establishing my own range of sauces and condiments.

Looking back now, I can see how much the Irish palate has changed and how it has adapted to Asian influences. When I arrived, it was all Uncle Ben's rice and jarred sauces. In the restaurant, customers regularly asked how 'spicy' a dish might be or would ask to have Asian words on the menu translated. Now my customers actively ask for my Asian sauces and condiments and are as comfortable with a rendang curry as they are with bacon and cabbage.

When I opened my first restaurant, The Cottage, in 2008, my aim was to combine the food of my childhood memories with the best Irish ingredients. The Cottage has weathered many storms – it literally flooded during the winters of 2010 and 2011 – recession and covid, but we've survived. The current menu is a tasting menu that features the best of local Irish produce with a distinctly Asian twist.

In 2013 I opened a café in Carrick-on-Shannon called Synergy, then in 2017 I became co-owner of a local steakhouse, Buffalo Boy, which takes its name from an old photo of my father sitting on a huge water buffalo.

During the covid lockdowns, I had time to focus on my more recent project – My Kitchen by Sham Hanifa, a larger café space that opened in October 2022 with a retail area and a dedicated space upstairs for cooking demonstrations. The menu features café classics and baked goods as well as dishes that reflect my background, such as the popular daily rice or noodle options, Thai-style salad bowls and always the rendang!

Ireland has been so good to me. People were friendly and welcoming and when I started out in my own business, I saw how loyal they were. I married an Irish girl and my two children are growing up fast, both working part time in the café but each with dreams of their own.

So much of my cooking is based on childhood memories – the tastes and aromas of home. I am delighted to share them with you in this book and I hope they bring you the same joy that they bring me.

THREE KEY INGREDIENTS

Malaysian food is a balance of sweet, salty, sour and spicy. We use a lot of chillies in our cooking, but the chilli heat sneaks in under the sugar so that it hits you pleasantly in the back of your throat rather than burning your lips. Lime leaves, ketjap manis and galangal are three ingredients that are key to Malaysian cooking that you might have to go out of your way to find, but it will be worth it. There are simply no substitutes for lime leaves and galangal.

1 FROZEN LIME LEAVES Lime leaves are one of those special ingredients that just can't be substituted. If you don't have them, it's better to leave them out altogether. Don't try to replace them with fresh lime or lemon because lime leaves add an intensity that nothing else can. But the good news is that you can buy frozen packs of them, so you can always have them on hand. Just take out however many you need for a recipe – you can slice them or add them to the dish straight from frozen.

2 KETJAP MANIS Also spelled kecap manis, this is an Indonesian sweet soy sauce. But don't be fooled, it's nothing like regular soy sauce. It's very thick and tastes like molasses or treacle, so either of those would be an acceptable substitute. There are many sweet soy sauces that are too sweet or too thick, but ketjap manis has the perfect consistency, so be sure to look for that specifically.

3 GALANGAL Galangal adds a beautiful floral smell and a sweet, earthy flavour in cooking. Like lime leaves, don't try to replace it with anything else if it's not available.

Lamb rendang

START HERE

SPICE PASTE #1 — LAMB RENDANG — BAO

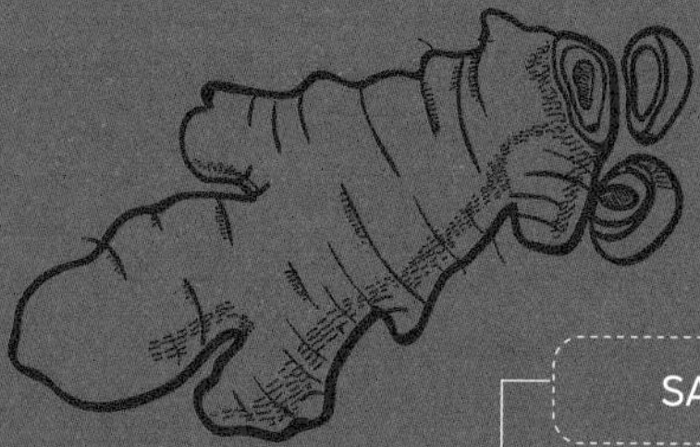

SPICE PASTE #2
- SATAY SAUCE
  - MALAYSIAN SPICY ROAST CHICKEN
  - CHICKEN OR BEEF SATAY SKEWERS
  - STUFFED TOFU
- MALAYSIAN SPICY ROAST CHICKEN
- CHICKEN OR BEEF SATAY SKEWERS
- CURRY CHICKEN KAPITAN — BAO

SPICE PASTE #3
- CHICKEN SAMBAL
  - SWEET & SOUR FISH
  - CHAR KWAY TEOW
  - KWAY TEOW KUNGFU
- SWEET & SOUR FISH
- CHAR KWAY TEOW

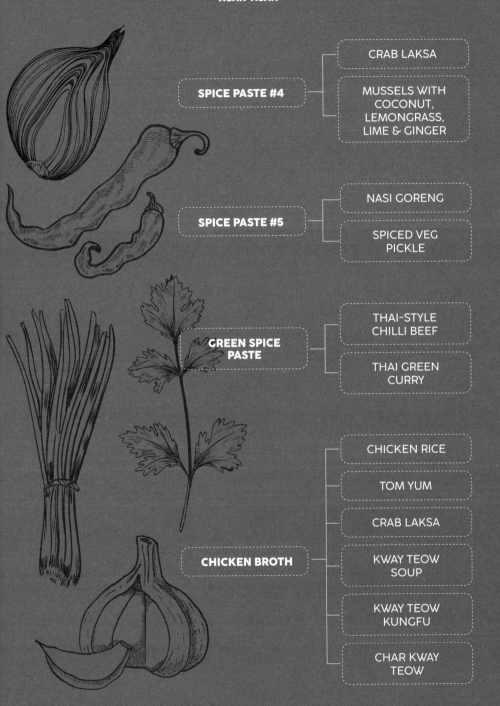

SPICE PASTE #4
- CRAB LAKSA
- MUSSELS WITH COCONUT, LEMONGRASS, LIME & GINGER

SPICE PASTE #5
- NASI GORENG
- SPICED VEG PICKLE

GREEN SPICE PASTE
- THAI-STYLE CHILLI BEEF
- THAI GREEN CURRY

CHICKEN BROTH
- CHICKEN RICE
- TOM YUM
- CRAB LAKSA
- KWAY TEOW SOUP
- KWAY TEOW KUNGFU
- CHAR KWAY TEOW

HOW TO MAKE

REMPAH (SPICE PASTE)

Rempah (spice paste) is often a combination of shallots, garlic, chillies, ginger, lemongrass, galangal and oil. I use these ingredients all the time in my curries, rendang, sambal, noodles and more. The rempah is the foundation of so many dishes in Malaysian cuisine – and lots of recipes in this book. It has the perfect balance of flavour to start off any of my cooking.

It's easy to prepare and convenient to have on hand. If you want to make it ahead or make a double batch, you can store the paste in a Kilner jar with a layer of oil on top in the fridge, like you'd store a pesto, for up to one week or you can freeze it in an ice cube tray, then pop the frozen cubes into a freezerproof bag. And by making a spice paste, none of the ingredients will go off and you won't be wasting any of them.

If you use a pestle and mortar to make your spice paste it will never be as smooth as it will be if you use a blender, but that's perfectly fine. If you need to loosen it in the blender to get the blades to catch the ingredients, use 1–2 tablespoons of oil, not water, because water will cause the paste to splatter when you add it to a hot pan.

I always try to get the balance of flavours right when I cook, which is why six different spice pastes are used in the recipes in this book. But if you've made a big batch of one of them or have one left over, then you could use them all interchangeably (except for the green spice paste) and the dish will still be delicious.

SPICE PASTE #1
MAKES 1 SMALL JAR

4 garlic cloves, chopped

3 shallots, chopped

3 fresh red chillies, chopped

2 lemongrass stalks, chopped

a thumb-sized piece of ginger, peeled and chopped

a thumb-sized piece of galangal, peeled and chopped (see page 4)

1 tbsp caster sugar

1 tbsp fine sea salt

Blend all the ingredients until smooth in a high-speed blender or crush them together in a pestle and mortar.

SPICE PASTE #2
MAKES 1 SMALL JAR

Add 1 tablespoon ground cumin, 1 tablespoon ground coriander and 1 tablespoon ground turmeric to spice paste #1.

SPICE PASTE #3
MAKES 1 SMALL JAR

8 shallots, roughly chopped

5 fresh red chillies, roughly chopped, seeds and all

4–5 garlic cloves, roughly chopped

4–5 lime leaves (see page 4)

2 lemongrass stalks, roughly chopped

a thumb-sized piece of fresh ginger, roughly chopped

Blend all the ingredients until smooth in a high-speed blender or crush them together in a pestle and mortar.

SPICE PASTE #4
MAKES 1 SMALL JAR

3 garlic cloves, chopped

2 lemongrass stalks, bottom halves only, thinly sliced (save the tops)

2 bird's eye chillies, chopped

2 thumb-sized pieces of ginger, roughly chopped

juice of 1 lime

1 tbsp fish sauce

1 tbsp water

1 tbsp ground turmeric

1 tsp ground coriander

Blend all the ingredients until smooth in a high-speed blender or crush them together in a pestle and mortar.

SPICE PASTE #5
MAKES 1 SMALL JAR

3 dried red chillies

3 shallots, roughly chopped

3 garlic cloves, roughly chopped

a thumb-sized piece of ginger, peeled and roughly chopped

1 tsp fine sea salt

1 tsp caster sugar

Soak the dried red chillies in a small bowl of water for 1 hour, until soft, then drain and roughly chop. Put the chillies in a pestle and mortar with the rest of the spice paste ingredients and crush to a paste. A blender won't work here – there are so few ingredients, they won't catch and blend properly.

GREEN SPICE PASTE
MAKES 1 X 400G JAR

Just use green chillies instead of red ones in spice paste #1 and add a large handful of fresh coriander (leaves and stems).

SATAY SAUCE

MAKES 1 LITRE

Satay sauce should be as thick as a jam, not runny. You dip food into it; it shouldn't be swimming in sauce. But Irish people have come to expect a thin, runny satay sauce, which is why in the Cottage Restaurant, we call it peanut jam to manage expectations and avoid confusion.

4–5 tbsp vegetable oil

1 shallot, finely diced

1 tsp grated garlic

3–5 tbsp spice paste #2 (page 8)

300g roasted, unsalted peanuts, coarsely crushed

2 x 400ml tins of full-fat coconut milk

50–100ml ketjap manis (see page 4)

1–2 tsp fine sea salt

1–3 tsp caster sugar

Heat 1 tablespoon of oil in a saucepan over a low heat. Add the shallot and garlic and cook for 1 minute, just until fragrant. Add the spice paste and cook for 2 minutes, stirring constantly. Stir in 3–4 more tablespoons of oil and continue to cook for a few minutes more. Don't be tempted to skip this extra oil! You need it to properly cook out all the raw ingredients in the spice paste.

Add the peanuts and cook, stirring, for 1 minute to toast them a little, then add the coconut milk, 50ml of the ketjap manis, 1 teaspoon of salt and 1 teaspoon of sugar. Simmer gently for 30 minutes, stirring occasionally so that it doesn't catch, until the oil separates out of the sauce and floats to the top and the sauce has reduced.

Taste the sauce and adjust the seasoning with more salt, sugar and/or ketjap manis. I often add another teaspoon of salt and sugar and up to 50ml of ketjap manis. Simmer for another 10–15 minutes, until the sauce is really thick, like a jam, and has turned a rich dark brown colour, almost like melted chocolate. You can tell a good satay by its colour – if it's too pale, you know it hasn't been simmered long enough.

Taste it one more time to adjust the sweetness with 1 more teaspoon of sugar if needed – when you taste this satay, you want your first impression to be sweet rather than salty.

CHICKEN BROTH

MAKES 2 LITRES

Along with the spice pastes, this broth is the hardest-working recipe in the book – it's used in the chicken rice (page 12), tom yum (page 36), crab laksa (page 40), kway teow soup (page 47) and char kway teow (page 50). Make life easy on yourself and make a double batch to freeze some.

1 x 1.1–1.5kg whole chicken

1 tbsp grated garlic

1 tbsp grated ginger

1 tbsp fine sea salt

Take your chicken out of the fridge and let it come up to room temperature before you start to cook. This is important so that there is less chance of the skin seizing up and slipping off when you add the chicken to the hot poaching water. Remove any excess fat from the bird (if you're making the chicken rice on page 12, finely chop the fat and set it aside).

To poach the chicken, put the garlic, ginger and salt in a large saucepan that will fit the whole chicken and fill the pan with plenty of cold water. Bring up to a simmer.

Use tongs to hold the chicken by its cavity over the pot. Using a ladle, baste it several times with the hot water. This will cause the skin to stick to the flesh – if you skip this step, the skin will slip right off from the shock of being dunked in the hot water. Lower the chicken into the pot and simmer, uncovered, for 60 minutes, until the chicken is fully cooked. You could reduce the broth at this point to give it a more intense flavour, but don't reduce it too much, otherwise it will be too salty.

Remove the chicken and use as needed for another recipe. The broth is now ready to use too.

HAINANESE NASI AYAM
CHICKEN RICE

SERVES 4

Why is this simple dish so good? My kids, my niece, my best man at my wedding and I all love it. Maybe it's the fact that it's so simple, but so full of flavour, that makes it so special. Hainanese chicken originated in the Hainan province in southern China. Brought over to Malaysia by the Chinese community, it's now served all over Asia. During lunchtime in any food court in Malaysia, chicken rice, as we call it, is very popular. A whole chicken is poached with ginger and garlic, then the rice is cooked in the resulting broth. The poached chicken can then either be brushed with sesame oil or glazed with honey and soy and briefly roasted to give it a beautiful golden brown colour. The rice is then served with the chopped chicken, a bowl of the chicken broth and sweet chilli dipping sauce.

1 whole poached chicken and all its broth (page 11), including the chicken fat

FOR THE RICE:

500g basmati rice

1 tbsp sesame oil, plus extra for brushing

1 tbsp grated garlic

½ tbsp grated ginger

1 tsp fine sea salt

TO FINISH THE BROTH:

1 spring onion, sliced at an angle

a thumb-sized piece of ginger, peeled and cut into matchsticks

a handful of roasted, unsalted peanuts

1 tsp fine sea salt

1 tsp caster sugar

Poach the chicken and make the broth as per the recipe on page 11, making sure you keep the chicken fat that you trim off the bird.

Meanwhile, soak the rice in a bowl of cold water for at least 30 minutes, then drain and rinse until the water runs clear.

Heat the sesame oil in a saucepan on a low heat. Finely chop the chicken fat and add it to the pan with the garlic and ginger and cook for 1 minute, until fragrant. Add the soaked, drained rice and stir to coat it in the fat and oil, then add 500ml of the chicken broth and the salt. Bring to a boil, then reduce the heat to its lowest setting, cover the pan with a tight-fitting lid and cook for about 15 minutes, until all the broth has been absorbed. Remove the pan from the heat and keep covered until you're ready to serve.

While the rice is cooking, make the sweet chilli dipping sauce by blitzing everything together in a high-speed blender.

To make the honey soy dipping sauce, whisk everything together in a small bowl.

You can either serve the chicken poached, just as it is and brushed with a little sesame oil to give it a nice flavour and shine, or you can roast it to burnish the skin. Or serve it both ways – use a cleaver or your sturdiest knife to cut the chicken in half along the breastbone and serve one half poached and the other half roasted. **>>**

FOR THE SWEET CHILLI DIPPING SAUCE:

200g fresh red chillies, roughly chopped

8 small garlic cloves (30g)

a thumb-sized piece of ginger

90g caster sugar

100ml distilled white vinegar

90ml lime juice

FOR THE HONEY SOY DIPPING SAUCE:

3 tbsp ketjap manis (see page 4)

2 tbsp honey

1 tbsp oyster sauce

If roasting, preheat the oven to 220°C (200°C fan). Put the chicken on a baking tray and brush it with some of the honey soy dipping sauce. Pour a ladleful of the broth into the tray so that the sauce doesn't burn. Roast the chicken in the oven for 15 minutes – it doesn't need long because it's already cooked; you're just getting some colour on it.

To finish, add the spring onion, ginger, peanuts, salt and sugar to the broth and bring it back to a simmer.

To serve, put each dipping sauce in a separate small bowl. Fluff up the rice with a fork and add a portion to each plate along with a small bowl of the broth. Carve the chicken and add it to the plate too – in Malaysia, it's traditionally cut straight across the bones. I like to drizzle a line of sweet chilli sauce and a line of the honey soy dipping sauce over the rice, then when it all gets too spicy, I take a break with a sip of broth.

COOK CLEVER
Use any leftover broth and chicken to make the kway teow soup on page 47. All the work is already done – all you have to do is cook a packet of noodles.

TRY THIS
To make this into a substantial soup in its own right, add some broth mix (a ready-to-go packet of barley, lentils and split peas that you can find in the health food aisle of the supermarket) to the broth along with leftover cooked chicken and diced veg that you've sautéed for 10–15 minutes.

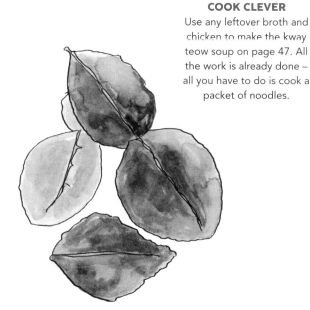

NASI GORENG
INDONESIAN FRIED RICE

SERVES 4

Every Malaysian grows up eating nasi goreng. The only difference is that we all have our own style of cooking it. The best way to make it is to use leftover rice. Malaysians eat rice every day, so we'd often have nasi goreng for breakfast or take a lunch box of nasi goreng to school. I always serve it with a sunny-side-up fried egg.

1 tbsp sesame oil

1 tbsp vegetable oil

1 shallot, sliced

1 garlic clove, sliced

1 batch of spice paste #5 (page 9)

1 tsp ground turmeric

4 boneless, skinless chicken thighs, diced very small (like for the satay skewers on pages 18–19)

2 tbsp ketjap manis (see page 4)

1 egg

600g leftover cooked basmati rice (or 200g dried rice, cooked as usual), not jasmine rice – it's too sticky

100g green beans, finely chopped

TO SERVE:
fried eggs, sunny side up

TO GARNISH:
thinly sliced spring onions

thinly sliced fresh red chilli

Heat the sesame and vegetable oils in a large wok or frying pan on a medium heat. Add the shallot and garlic and cook for 1 minute, until fragrant, then add the spice paste. Cook for 1–2 minutes, stirring, then add the turmeric and cook for 1 minute.

Add the chicken, stirring to coat it all with the paste. Cook for a few minutes, then add the ketjap manis. Stir-fry for another minute or two, then crack in the egg and quickly scramble it, stirring constantly.

Add the cooked rice and green beans and cook for 5 minutes to thoroughly heat the rice until it's piping hot and has absorbed all the flavours. Spread it out evenly in the wok or pan so that it dries out evenly – this makes it less stodgy. Taste and season with salt.

Divide among bowls, serve with a fried egg, sunny side up, and garnish with thinly sliced spring onion and chilli.

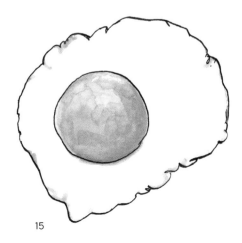

NASI LEMAK
COCONUT RICE

SERVES 4

In Malaysia, you can have nasi lemak for breakfast with sambal, hardboiled eggs, cucumber, fried anchovies and peanuts, all wrapped in banana leaves and newspaper to have on the go if you're in a hurry to get to work or school. The creaminess of the coconut milk makes the rice a little sticky, which works well to bind all the other ingredients you might want to add to it. Nasi lemak is also served at many special occasions with rendang, especially during the festive season or at a wedding. My personal favourite is coconut rice served with prawn sambal.

500g basmati rice

2 thumb-sized pieces of ginger, peeled and cut into matchsticks

2–3 fresh pandan leaves, tied into a knot

2 x 400ml tins of full-fat coconut milk

200ml water

1 tbsp fine sea salt

1 tbsp caster sugar

Soak the rice in a bowl of cold water for at least 30 minutes, then drain and rinse until the water runs clear.

Pop everything into a rice cooker if you have one and cook according to the manufacturer's instructions. If cooking on the hob, put everything in a medium-sized saucepan and bring to a boil, then cover with a tight-fitting lid, reduce the heat to the lowest possible setting and cook for 30–45 minutes, until all the liquid has been absorbed.

To serve, discard the pandan leaves and fluff up the rice with a fork.

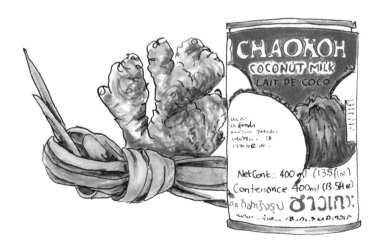

AYAM PERCIK
MALAYSIAN SPICY ROAST CHICKEN

SERVES 4

This is authentic Malay street food at its best. During Ramadan in particular, you can see all the locals out in the evening or at the night market after breaking their fast to shop for the best ayam percik. Every stall has their own special version of this dish, whether it's the way they marinate the chicken or the way they make their satay sauce, but the one thing they all have in common is that when you're in the market and you can smell the chicken being grilled from a distance, it makes you want to go there and buy it.

4 bone-in, skin-on chicken legs

juice of 1 lime

3 tbsp spice paste #2 (page 8)

1 tbsp light brown sugar

4 tbsp satay sauce (page 10)

Score the skin on the chicken legs a few times, then put the chicken in a large bowl with the lime juice, spice paste and brown sugar. Massage everything into the skin, cover the bowl with cling film and marinate in the fridge overnight.

Preheat the oven to 200°C (180°C fan). Line a baking tray with non-stick baking paper.

Put the chicken on the lined tray, making sure you include every bit of marinade from the bowl so that the legs are thickly coated with it.

Cook in the oven for 20 minutes, then increase the temperature to 220°C (200°C fan) and cook for 20 minutes more, until the chicken is completely cooked through and getting charred.

Brush each leg with 1 tablespoon of the satay sauce, then return to the oven to cook for a few minutes more, until sticky, deep golden-brown and burnished.

SATAY AYAM OR SATAY DAGING
CHICKEN OR BEEF SATAY SKEWERS

MAKES 8–10 SKEWERS

Kajang is a town that's renowned for its satay. Years ago, people would travel to Kajang just to get the best satay in the area. It became so famous and in demand that people started to copy their name and suddenly satay kajang started popping up in every town and city in Malaysia. But nothing compares to the original satay kajang when you go to the actual town.

If you visit family or friends in Malaysia, it's common to get a dozen of each skewer to bring to the house you're visiting. Nothing beats having a satay and chat outside the house for a bit of gossip.

4 boneless, skinless chicken thighs or 500g beef fillet or sirloin

1 batch of spice paste #2 (page 8)

1 batch of satay sauce (page 10)

If you're using wooden skewers, soak them in water for at least 30 minutes so they don't burn when you grill them.

Cut the chicken or beef into very thin slices, then cut again into 2cm square pieces. The meat needs to be cut very small because it cooks so quickly. Put the meat in a bowl and toss with 2–3 tablespoons of the spice paste, then thread the pieces onto 8–10 skewers. If you're using beef, keep the pieces as flat as possible on the skewer. Chicken will naturally be more bunched up.

Marinate chicken skewers in the fridge for no longer than 4–6 hours and beef skewers for 2 hours max, otherwise the flavour of the spice paste will overpower the meat.

Meanwhile, make the satay as per the recipe on page 10 but use the remaining spice paste left over here from marinating the meat rather than the full batch called for in the master recipe. Keep warm.

When you're ready to cook, get a ridged grill pan smoking hot. Working in batches, add the skewers to the hot pan. Leave them alone for 2–3 minutes without touching or moving them to let them develop a nice char. Flip over and cook for another 2–3 minutes for beef skewers or 4–5 minutes for chicken, until the meat is completely cooked through.

To serve, lightly brush each skewer with satay sauce, then serve extra satay in a ramekin on the side for dipping.

TOP TIPS

Making good satay skewers comes down to a few key details:

1 If you're using wooden skewers, soaking them is essential so they won't burn when you grill them.

2 I always use chicken thighs because the fat from the thighs gives the skewers a better flavour. If you want to use a cheaper bit of beef fillet, ask your butcher for the fillet head or fillet tail. These are the trimmings of the more expensive tenderloin but still have all the tenderness and flavour of fillet.

3 The meat needs to be cut very small because it cooks so quickly. Cutting the meat this small is the most time-consuming part of this recipe. In Malaysia, the thinner the chicken, the more expensive the skewer is because of the extra time and work involved in making it. If you see skewers with big chunks of chicken, you know the cook got impatient!

4 Marinate the meat in the spice paste to let it absorb all the flavours.

5 Traditionally, these are grilled over an open charcoal fire as street food. The combination of coconut milk, sugar and oil will create a spark of fire that will give the meat a good char – and the char is what really makes this dish.

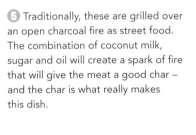

CHICKEN SAMBAL

SERVES 4

Sambal is a Malaysian favourite and a must-have celebratory dish for special occasions. At my sister's wedding, my father's friends set up their cooking equipment outside the house and cooked it for the 500 people who came that day.

Growing up in Taiping, when we went to school in the morning, we would get nasi lemak (coconut rice) in our school canteen with a choice of prawn sambal, chicken sambal, squid sambal, anchovy sambal and many more. Sambal is usually served with nasi lemak (page 16) because the creaminess of the coconut is the perfect complement to the spicy, sweet and sour flavour of the sambal. Every mouthful fills you with joy. The spices dance in your mouth and you can't stop going back for more.

3 tbsp vegetable oil

1 batch of spice paste #3 (page 9)

1 tsp ground turmeric

3 lime leaves, shredded (see page 4)

5 tbsp soy sauce

1 tbsp fish sauce

200ml water

6 boneless, skinless chicken thighs, diced

juice of 1 lime

2 tbsp light brown sugar

200g green beans, cut into three or four pieces

FOR THE TAMARIND JUICE:

45g tamarind pulp

300ml water

TO SERVE:

nasi lemak (page 16)

To make the tamarind juice, soak the tamarind pulp in the water until the pulp has dissolved.

Meanwhile, heat the oil in a large wok or frying pan on a medium heat. Add the spice paste (see the cook clever tip) and cook for 5 minutes, stirring. Add the turmeric and cook for another 5 minutes, still stirring, until the paste has darkened in colour and the raw ingredients are all cooked.

Add two-thirds of the lime leaves and all the tamarind juice and simmer for a few minutes, then add 1 tablespoon of soy sauce, the fish sauce and the water. Stir in the chicken and bring to a boil, then reduce the heat and simmer for 10–15 minutes, until the chicken is cooked.

Add the lime juice, 1 tablespoon of sugar and another 2 tablespoons of soy sauce to balance the sweetness. Cook for 10 minutes, until the sauce has reduced slightly and the oil has separated out of the sauce around the edges of the pan. It will look like a lot of oil, but don't worry!

Add the green beans and cook for a few minutes, then finish with a final tablespoon of sugar, the remaining 2 tablespoons of soy sauce and the rest of the lime leaves. The sambal should have a good balance of sourness, saltiness and sweetness.

Divide the sambal among bowls and serve with nasi lemak (coconut rice) on the side.

COOK CLEVER
Keep back 2 tablespoons of the spice paste
to make the sweet and sour fish on page 44
or 1 tablespoon for the char kway teow on
page 50. Keep 200ml of the broth to make
the kway teow kungfu on page 48.

CHICKEN
AND BEEF
SATAY
SKEWERS

COCONUT
RICE

CHICKEN
SAMBAL

TOP TIP
You could add veg to this recipe, but
the moisture in vegetables throws off
the balance of flavours. That's why in
Malaysia, we almost always serve veg
plain on the side or as a slaw.

GAI PRIK
BLACK PEPPER CHICKEN SKEWERS

MAKES 4 SKEWERS

This is my Thai grandmother's all-time favourite recipe, but she makes it with beef. She passed it on to my mother and now to me. We ate this a lot when we couldn't afford to go shopping or when we wanted to use what we had in the house, since we could get the chicken or beef from my dad, who was a butcher. It's a simple recipe with a few key ingredients. Garlic adds a nice earthy flavour, soy sauce adds saltiness, sugar adds sweetness and caramelisation, and the black pepper adds a gentle heat.

2 tbsp coarsely ground black pepper

2 tbsp light brown sugar

3 tbsp Kikkoman soy sauce

1 tbsp grated garlic

4 boneless, skinless chicken thighs, each cut into thirds (or beef fillet or sirloin, thinly sliced and cut into bite-sized pieces)

4 spring onions, white and light green parts cut into pieces 3cm long (ideally the same size as the chicken strips)

vegetable oil, for brushing

TO SERVE:

som tam (page 60) or watermelon slices

Put the black pepper, sugar, soy sauce and garlic in a medium-sized bowl and whisk to combine, then add the chicken strips and toss to coat. Cover and marinate in the fridge for 2–3 hours at most (or 1 hour max if using beef). Don't let it marinate for too long because the saltiness of the soy sauce will start to overpower the meat.

Meanwhile, if you're using wooden skewers, soak them in cold water so they don't burn on the pan. Alternatively, you don't need to use skewers at all – you could pan fry the chicken just as it is.

When you're ready to assemble, start each skewer with a spring onion, then add a piece of chicken. The key to these skewers is making sure the chicken isn't overlapping on itself anywhere on the skewer, as that means it won't cook through properly – you need to keep the pieces as flat as possible on the skewer. Alternate so that you have four pieces of spring onion and three pieces of chicken on each skewer, starting and ending with spring onion.

Put a griddle pan or a large non-stick frying pan on a high heat (or cooking them on a barbecue would be even better). Brush the skewers with oil. Working in batches if necessary so that you don't crowd the pan, add the skewers to the hot pan and cook for 1½–2 minutes without touching or moving them so that they get a nice char. Flip over and cook for 1½–2 minutes more,

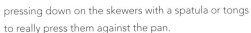

pressing down on the skewers with a spatula or tongs to really press them against the pan.

Now flip the skewers every 30 seconds or so until they have cooked for 6 minutes in total or until the chicken is fully cooked through. Once you've achieved a good char from the initial cooking, you can turn the heat down to get the chicken to cook through evenly. If you're pan-frying the chicken instead of using skewers, you need to keep a closer eye on it, as it will cook more quickly than the skewers and you don't want it to burn.

Serve the skewers with a cooling side of som tam (mango and papaya slaw) or watermelon slices.

CHICKEN MURTABAK

SERVES 4

This Malaysian street food is served all day. Cooked, diced chicken is bound together with eggs, then spooned onto roti, folded into a square pastry and fried on a flat cast iron pan until it's crisp all over.

Whenever I went to meet my dad at his butcher shop (usually looking for few quid to buy football gear), I would be sent to the hawker stall next door to wait to see him. It was a meeting point or place to go for breakfast or lunch for the butchers. We would always order chicken murtabak, served with a bit of curry sauce and pickled red onion.

1 batch of roti canai dough (page 57)

2 tbsp vegetable oil, plus extra to cook

1 red onion, finely diced

2 tsp fine sea salt

2 tbsp Baba's Meat Curry Powder (see the note) or any good-quality curry powder

4–5 chicken fillets, minced or very finely chopped

1 tsp caster sugar

2 eggs, beaten

4 knobs of butter

TO SERVE:

acar berempah (page 62)

sambal oelek

The roti dough needs to rest overnight, so make that the day before you want to make this dish.

When you're ready to cook, take the roti dough out of the fridge to let it come up to room temperature.

Heat the oil in a large frying pan on a medium heat. Add the red onion and salt and cook for 5–8 minutes, until softened. Add the curry powder and cook for 1 minute, then add the chicken and sugar and cook, constantly stirring and mashing, for 5–7 minutes, until cooked through. Tip the mixture out into a bowl and allow to cool, then mix in the eggs along with another pinch of salt to bind it all together.

Stretch out the roti dough as outlined on pages 57–59 but don't fold in the edges of the dough yet.

Heat 1 tablespoon of oil in a large non-stick frying pan on a medium-low heat. Working with one stretched-out ball of dough at a time, put 2–3 tablespoons of the chicken filling in the middle. Using the back of a spoon, spread it out in an even, single layer that's roughly square shaped. Fold the edges of the dough over the filling to completely enclose it.

Gently lift the filled dough off the countertop and flip it into the hot pan, seam side down. Cook for 2–3 minutes, until golden, then flip it over and cook for 2–3 minutes more, until the filling is piping hot and the eggs are cooked through.

BABA'S MEAT CURRY POWDER

For me, this dish doesn't taste quite right unless I use Baba's Meat Curry Powder (aka the green one). Baba's is a brand that you can get at Asian shops but if you can't find it, use your own favourite curry powder. Just make sure it's a good-quality one so it will have a nice balance of spices.

Press down on it with a fish slice as it cooks – if any moisture leaks out, you know the eggs haven't cooked through yet. Sometimes if the pan gets too hot I sprinkle in a little water to reduce the heat and also because it helps to develop the charred flavour.

Once both sides are golden brown, continue to cook, flipping it over every minute or so, to deepen the colour and make sure the bread is cooked through, with no pockets of raw dough.

Add a knob of butter to the pan and allow it to melt over the murtabak. Slide it out onto a chopping board and cut in half or into soldiers to serve. Repeat with the remaining dough and filling.

Serve warm with acar berempah and sambal oelek on the side.

KARI KAPITAN
CURRY CHICKEN KAPITAN

SERVES 4

There are different versions of the origins of this dish. I've been told it comes from the Chinese Baba-Nyonya community in Melaka, who started cooking this dish for the captains of the Portuguese ships that would pass through the city heading to Australia during the colonial period. When the curry was ready to be served, the cook would say, 'Your kari, kapitan.'

When I would visit my Aunty Chit (my mother's eldest sister) and her Chinese husband, my Uncle William Ang, during Lunar New Year, she always cooked this dish. On arrival to their house we looked forward to meeting him first because he would be sitting on the sofa in the corner with his glass of XO and red envelopes filled with money. We had to shake his hand and wish him a happy new year and lots of prosperity and happiness before he would give us the envelopes. Then we would all sit down and eat the kari kapitan.

40g tamarind pulp

200ml cold water

1 tbsp vegetable oil

1 garlic clove, thinly sliced

4–5 lime leaves, shredded (see page 4)

2 red onions, halved and thinly sliced

1 tbsp Baba's Meat Curry Powder (see the note on page 25)

2 tbsp spice paste #2 (page 8)

500g boneless, skinless chicken thighs, diced

1 Maris Piper potato, peeled and cubed

juice of 1 lime

½ x 400ml tin of coconut milk (see the note)

1 tbsp caster sugar

1 tsp fine sea salt

Soak the tamarind pulp in the cold water until it has dissolved.

Heat the oil in a large saucepan or wok on a medium heat. Add the garlic and most of the shredded lime leaves and cook for 30 seconds, until fragrant. Add the onions and cook for 2 minutes, then add the curry powder and cook it off for 1 minute. Add the spice paste and cook for a few minutes, until the oil separates out.

Add the chicken and stir to coat. Cook for a few minutes, then add the potato and lime juice and pour in the tamarind juice, making sure you don't get any of the pulp in the dish if it hasn't all completely dissolved. Bring to a boil, then reduce the heat. Simmer for 10–15 minutes, uncovered, until the chicken and potato are cooked through, the sauce has reduced by half and the oil has separated out and is floating on the surface. Kapitan has a drier, thicker consistency than other curries. It's richer and full of flavour from the curry spice, the lemongrass, chilli and ginger from the spice paste, and a bit of sourness from the tamarind and lime. During this cooking process, the key is to be patient and allow all the flavours to be absorbed into the chicken.

SHOP SMART

If you're shopping in an Asian market, look for small 200ml or 165ml tins of coconut milk. They're handy for recipes like this one that don't need a full tin.

Stir in the coconut milk and simmer for 5 minutes, then add the sugar and salt and simmer for 5 minutes more, until the sauce has reduced right down and is quite thick.

Ladle into wide, deep bowls, garnish with the remaining shredded lime leaves and serve with any kind of bread.

BEE HOON SOUP
BEEF NOODLE BROTH

SERVES 4

Even though Malaysia is a warm country, we love this soup. After a busy night of service, my friends and I would go to Kampung Baru, a village in the heart of Kuala Lumpur's central business district that has held on to its rural atmosphere, to order bee hoon soup from a night market hawker's stall. This warm, hearty dish of beef brisket or beef chuck cooked on the bone with cinnamon, star anise, cardamom, cloves and garlic, served with vermicelli rice noodles and vegetables, was the perfect dish to relax and wind down with. These days, when I come in from the cold after playing a round of golf, this is what I want to eat. I also serve this at My Kitchen in Carrick-on-Shannon during the winter, where it's a popular dish with the locals.

FOR THE BROTH:

5 litres cold water

3 big beef short ribs, preferably a Jacob's ladder cut (1.2kg), or 6 small short ribs

6–7 shallots, sliced

6 garlic cloves, sliced

4 celery sticks, sliced

4 spring onions, sliced

a thumb-sized piece of ginger, peeled and sliced

8 cloves

8 green cardamom pods

4 star anise

2 cinnamon sticks

2 tsp ground black pepper

1 tbsp fine sea salt

1 tbsp caster sugar

Fill a large pot with the water. Add the beef and slowly bring up to a simmer to render out the fat, then skim off as much of the fat and froth that rises to the top as you can. If you let the water vigorously boil, it will be harder to capture that foam and fat because it will be going all over the place. Don't be tempted to skip this step because if you leave the fat in, every mouthful of the broth will feel greasy on your lips.

Remove the beef and gently rinse it off, then return it to the pot along with the veg, spices and black pepper. Bring to a boil, then reduce to a simmer and cook, uncovered, for 1½ hours, until the beef is tender and you've extracted all the flavour out of the aromatics. Halfway through the cooking time, add the salt and sugar. You want to simmer the broth until it has reduced by 40–50% and is deeply flavourful. Don't reduce it any more than this, though, or the broth will get too strong and concentrated.

When the broth is nearly ready, cook the noodles according to the packet instructions, then drain and set aside.

Remove the pot from the heat. Transfer the beef to a plate and strain the stock through a fine mesh sieve, then discard the solids. (For me, there's nothing worse than biting into a whole star anise or clove.) Cut the beef away from the bones

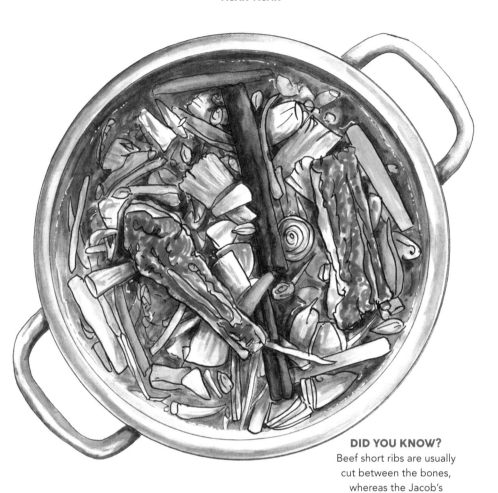

DID YOU KNOW?
Beef short ribs are usually cut between the bones, whereas the Jacob's ladder leaves them whole, typically with three to five rib bones in one long piece.

TO FINISH:

400g rice vermicelli noodles

crispy shallots

thinly sliced fresh red chilli

fresh coriander leaves

a handful of beansprouts

and trim off and discard any fat, then thinly slice the beef.

To serve, divide the noodles and beef among four wide, deep bowls. Ladle over the broth and garnish with crispy shallots, sliced fresh chilli, fresh coriander leaves and beansprouts.

PHAD PHRIK
THAI-STYLE CHILLI BEEF

SERVES 4

For me, this recipe is a mama and abah (mom and dad) combination. On the days we did our grocery shopping, we'd head to town for a treat and the shop, then meet my dad and get some beef from his butcher shop so my mum could cook this dish. The green chillies, garlic, lime leaves and green beans all came from our back garden. My mum uses green bird's eye chillies but I don't recommend it! They will burn your mouth or make you sweat if you're not used to them. I've adapted her recipe a bit so it's not too spicy.

2 tbsp vegetable oil

2–3 garlic cloves, thinly sliced

6 tbsp green spice paste (page 9)

1 tbsp coarsely ground black pepper

600g beef fillet, thinly sliced

3 tbsp fish sauce

100ml water

6 lime leaves (see page 4), shredded, plus extra to garnish

1 tbsp light brown sugar, plus extra to taste

100g green beans, chopped

juice of 1 lime

½ tsp fine sea salt or to taste

Heat 1 tablespoon of oil in a large frying pan on a medium heat. Add the garlic and cook for 1 minute, just until fragrant. Add the spice paste and cook it off for a few minutes, until the oil separates out of the paste, stirring constantly so that it cooks evenly.

Stir in the remaining tablespoon of oil along with the black pepper. Keep cooking until the oil splits out of the spice paste again and the colour darkens, then add the beef. Cook for a few minutes to coat it in the paste, stirring constantly, then add 1 tablespoon of fish sauce and cook for 5 minutes, still stirring.

Add the water, half of the lime leaves, the sugar and the remaining 2 tablespoons of fish sauce and let it all bubble up. Keep simmering until the oil splits out of the sauce again. The reason you want the oil to keep separating out from the sauce is because that's when you know the spices have bound to the meat, almost like glue. Otherwise, you'll just be leaving all that flavour in the pan! You're looking for all the sauce to cling to the meat the way a carbonara sauce should all stick to the pasta – you don't want it to be runny. Keep cooking until it's impossible to separate the sauce from the meat because it's so reduced and thick. Be patient and hold your nerve!

Add the green beans and the remaining lime leaves. Cook for just 2 minutes, stirring, until the beans are bright green

TRY THIS
If this turns out too spicy for you, just stir in some coconut milk at the end to temper the heat and turn this into a Thai green curry.

and still have some crunch. Stir in the lime juice, then taste and adjust the seasoning with more sugar and salt if needed – I usually add ½ teaspoon of each at this stage.

To serve, divide among bowls and garnish with extra shredded lime leaves.

PHAD GRA POW
THAI BASIL BEEF

SERVES 4

When I was growing up, my Thai grandparents lived with us until I was 13 years old. My grandmother was a cook at the Buddhist temple, where she cooked for the monks and visitors. She made this dish with pork but my mother uses the best bit of beef she can get instead. It always brings back memories of my childhood for me.

FOR THE MARINADE:

2 tbsp soy sauce

1 tsp grated garlic

1 tsp light brown sugar

1 tsp ground black pepper

500g beef fillet, sliced very thinly

TO COOK:

2 tbsp vegetable oil

2 garlic cloves, thinly sliced

a thumb-sized piece of ginger, peeled and thinly sliced

1 shallot, thinly sliced

1 fresh red chilli, thinly sliced at an angle

1 tsp ground black pepper

2 tbsp oyster sauce

1 tbsp soy sauce

2 tbsp water

1 tsp light brown sugar

1 tsp slaked cornflour (i.e. cornflour mixed with a little liquid)

a handful of fresh Thai basil leaves

TO SERVE:

boiled basmati rice

Mix together the soy sauce, garlic, sugar and pepper. Put the beef in a shallow bowl or baking dish and pour over the marinade. Set aside for just 15 minutes while you prepare the rest of the ingredients.

Put a dry wok or a large frying pan on a high heat and let it get really hot – don't add any oil. Add the beef and stir-fry for 1 minute, then push it to the sides of the wok or pan to keep the middle clear.

Add the oil, garlic and ginger and stir-fry for 30 seconds. Add the shallot, chilli and black pepper, then mix the beef back in. Stir-fry for another 30 seconds, then add the oyster sauce and soy sauce. Cook for 1–2 minutes, then pour in the water to dilute the saltiness. Let it bubble up and reduce, then stir in the sugar, cornflour and most of the basil. Cook until the sauce thickens and coats the beef.

Serve with boiled basmati rice and garnish with the remaining whole basil leaves.

LAMB RENDANG

SERVES 4

The origins of this dish are up for debate. Indonesia lays claim to it but so does Malaysia. One thing both versions have in common, though, is the careful use of spices to create a perfect balance of flavour.

Rendang is a celebratory dish in Malaysian culture. It makes me smile every time I make it, from the aroma of the spices when I start to cook it until I sit down to eat it. What can I say? I love rendang!

At my sister's wedding, my father's friends cooked chicken sambal (page 20) and rendang outside the house for the hundreds of invited guests. The process started hours before the reception so that the rendang could slow-cook in 100-litre pots, so can you imagine how incredible our neighbourhood smelled!

This dish is made in two stages. In the first stage, you're binding the spices to the meat before you braise it in the second stage. It simmers slowly at each stage, like you would do if you were making a traditional Bolognese sauce. You can use any meat in this rendang – in Malaysia, we use lamb, mutton, beef, buffalo or chicken – just adjust the cooking time accordingly. You need to be patient when cooking this dish, as you need to give it time to pack in all the flavour. But trust me, it's worth it.

50ml vegetable oil

5 cloves

4 star anise

1 lemongrass stalk, bruised and cut in half across its width

1 large cinnamon stick, broken in half

3–4 shallots, roughly chopped

2 tbsp Baba's Meat Curry Powder (see the note on page 25)

1 batch of spice paste #1 (page 8)

1kg diced lamb shoulder

To temper the spices, heat the oil in a large saucepan on a medium heat. Add the cloves, star anise, bruised lemongrass and the cinnamon stick. Cook for 1–2 minutes, until fragrant.

Add the shallots and cook for a few minutes, until starting to soften, then add the curry powder and cook it off for 30 seconds before you add the spice paste. Cook, stirring occasionally, for about 5 minutes, until the oil starts to separate out of the spice paste. This is the foundation of all the flavour in this dish, so take your time to get it right.

Add the lamb, stirring to coat it in the paste. Fry for 5–10 minutes to bind the spices to the meat and to separate out the oil again (the fat in the lamb will also render out).

Stir in 1 tablespoon of ketjap manis and cook for 5 minutes, then add 1 tablespoon of sugar and 1 tablespoon of salt.

2 tbsp ketjap manis (see page 4)

3 tbsp caster sugar

2 tbsp fine sea salt

500ml water

6–7 lime leaves, shredded (see page 4)

1 x 400ml tin of full-fat coconut milk

200g desiccated coconut, toasted

TO GARNISH:

thinly sliced fresh red chilli

fresh coriander leaves

TO SERVE:

nasi lemak (page 16)

Add the water and half of the shredded lime leaves. Bring up to a simmer and cook for 30 minutes, uncovered, until the sauce has reduced by half and the lamb is halfway cooked through, stirring occasionally so it doesn't stick. The rendang will look very oily, but this is what you want so don't worry.

Add the coconut milk along with another tablespoon of ketjap manis, sugar and salt. Simmer for another 30 minutes, until the sauce has reduced by half again and the oil has separated out again.

Add the toasted desiccated coconut and another tablespoon of sugar. There should now be lots of oil floating on top and the lamb should be well coated in the paste, which should now look quite chunky. Stir in the remaining lime leaves.

To serve, divide the rendang among wide, shallow bowls with a slotted spoon to leave as much of the oil behind as possible. Garnish with sliced red chillies and coriander leaves and serve with nasi lemak (coconut rice).

COOK CLEVER
Use leftovers in a bao bun (page 54) – a little goes a long way.

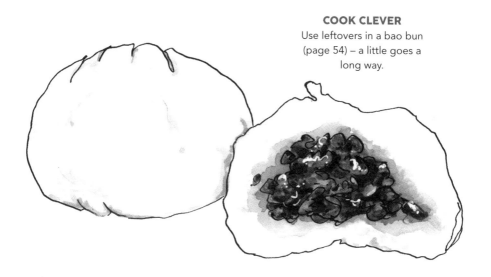

TOM YUM

SERVES 4

My Thai grandmother, Mae Thau, is the master of tom yum (tom = boiled and yum = spice). Her version is different than any other tom yum I've ever tasted. Her recipe is also the steamboat version, where the broth is served in a special bowl in the centre, with separate bowls of prawns, chicken, shellfish and vegetables circling it. You add whatever you like to the boiling broth to heat it up, then pour it into your bowl and serve it with rice or noodles.

This is a clear broth, whereas you might be familiar with tom yum that has a red colour – that version is made with a paste. The broth of this homemade soup isn't oily either, as there is no oil in the recipe.

FOR THE BROTH:

1 litre chicken broth (page 11 or a well-flavoured broth or stock) or fish stock

2 garlic cloves, thinly sliced

2 lemongrass stalks, bruised and cut in half

2 bird's eye chillies, cut in half lengthways

6 lime leaves (see page 4)

a thumb-sized piece of galangal, sliced (see page 4)

juice of 2 limes

1 tbsp fish sauce

1 tsp fine sea salt

1 tsp caster sugar

a handful of fresh coriander

Put all the broth ingredients except the coriander in a large saucepan on a medium heat. Do not boil, otherwise the broth will turn cloudy. Just let it gently simmer for 15–20 minutes to extract all the flavours without reducing.

Add the handful of coriander and simmer for a few minutes more, then bring to a boil. Immediately strain into a clean saucepan through a fine mesh sieve, but I like to return the lemongrass and lime leaves to the strained broth. Some people don't strain the broth, but I find it too difficult to eat otherwise. Discard the solids.

Add all the finishing ingredients to the strained broth and bring back up to a simmer. Cook for only 3 minutes, just until the prawns are cooked through. Don't allow it to simmer for too long at this stage or the lime juice will lose its freshness and become bitter and the chillies will become too intense. You want to keep the delicate, fresh balance of flavours.

To serve, divide among four wide, deep bowls. Garnish with fresh coriander leaves and squeeze over a lime wedge for a final burst of freshness.

TO FINISH:

12 fresh prawns, shelled
and deveined

4 oyster or button
mushrooms, thinly sliced

1 shallot, halved lengthways
and thinly sliced

1 small ripe tomato, cut into
4–6 wedges

2–3 lime leaves, shredded

1 tsp fine sea salt

1 tsp caster sugar

TO GARNISH:

fresh coriander leaves

lime wedges

MAE THAU, MY THAI GRANDMOTHER, IS A LEGEND – AND THE BEST COOK. SHE WAS THE HIGHLY REGARDED COOK AT THE BUDDHIST TEMPLE, WHERE OVER THE YEARS SHE COOKED FOR THOUSANDS OF PEOPLE, INCLUDING MY GRANDFATHER WHEN HE WAS A MONK THERE.

she makes the best authentic Thai crab laksa.

MY MOTHER TOLD ME THAT WHEN MAE THAU USED TO SELL LAKSA AT A STREET HAWKER STALL IN HER FREE TIME, SHE WOULD ALWAYS SELL OUT BEFORE NOON.

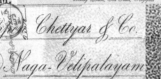

MY FATHER WAS A
BODYGUARD FOR THE PERAK
PRINCE AT THE TIME AND HE
USED TO GET HER TO COOK
THE CRAB LAKSA TO BRING TO
THE PRINCE AT THE PALACE.

*we were so spoiled
when she made it for us
when she lived with us.*

CRAB LAKSA

SERVES 4

When I was in Hat Yai in Thailand recently, I came across a stall selling crab laksa. I stopped straight away to try it and my memories of Mae Thau's dish came flooding back.

1kg cooked crab claws

1 tbsp vegetable oil

1 batch of spice paste #4 (page 9), plus the reserved lemongrass tops

FOR THE BROTH:

1 litre chicken broth (page 11 or a well-flavoured broth or stock)

3–4 lime leaves, torn (see page 4)

1 tbsp fine sea salt

1 tbsp caster sugar

1 tbsp fish sauce

2 x 400ml tins of full-fat coconut milk

200ml water

1 tbsp light brown sugar

TO FINISH:

200g thick, flat rice noodles (10mm)

200g vermicelli rice noodles

Cook the thick and vermicelli rice noodles in separate pots according to the packet instructions. Drain and set aside.

Tip the crab claws into a large hot, dry wok or frying pan set on a high heat. Cook for 10 minutes, tossing now and then, to heat them up and intensify their flavour.

Add the oil, stirring to coat the crab claws, then add the spice paste (see the tip on the next page) and stir to coat again. Cook for 1–2 minutes.

Add the chicken broth, lime leaves, salt, sugar and fish sauce. Bring to a boil, then lower the heat and simmer until reduced by half.

Stir in the coconut milk, water and brown sugar and add the remaining lemongrass halves reserved from the spice paste. Simmer to heat the coconut milk but don't let it reduce.

To serve, divide the cooked noodles among four wide, deep bowls. Ladle over the broth and crab claws, then let everyone add their own garnishes.

TO GARNISH:
fresh Thai basil

fresh mint

fresh coriander leaves

thinly sliced fresh red chilli

a handful of beansprouts

lime wedges

COOK CLEVER
Reserve 1 tablespoon of
the spice paste and use it
to make the mussels with
coconut, lemongrass, lime
and ginger on page 43.

MUSSELS WITH COCONUT, LEMONGRASS, LIME & GINGER

SERVES 4

Living in Ireland for the past 23 years, I've had the chance to travel all over the country with Euro-Toques to see and taste the best of Irish produce, including a boat trip in the Killary fjord to taste beautiful Irish mussels. With my Asian background, I love to create East-meets-West dishes like this one. Originally this masak lemak recipe uses clams, cockles or periwinkles but I decided to use mussels. It's simple and quick to prepare if you already have the spice paste in the fridge or freezer. Just fry the paste to bring up the aroma, then add the coconut milk and mussels and it's ready in no time.

1kg mussels

1 tbsp vegetable oil

1 shallot, halved lengthways and thinly sliced

1 garlic clove, thinly sliced

1 bird's eye chilli, halved lengthways

1 lemongrass stalk, bruised

1 tbsp spice paste #4 (page 9)

50ml water

1 x 400ml tin of full-fat coconut milk

juice of ½ lime

1 lime leaf

1 tbsp fish sauce, plus extra to taste

1 tsp light brown sugar

Rinse the mussels under cold running water and debeard them. If any are open, give them a gentle tap on the countertop. If they close, they're safe to eat. If they stay open, throw them away.

Heat the oil in a large saucepan on a medium heat. Add the shallot, garlic, chilli, lemongrass and spice paste. Cook for 1 minute, then add the water and cook for 30 seconds before stirring in the coconut milk. Bring up to a simmer, then add the lime juice, lime leaf, fish sauce and brown sugar.

Add the mussels, cover the pan and give it a quick shake. Cook for 3 minutes, until all the mussels have opened. Discard any that are still closed. Taste the sauce and adjust the seasoning with more fish sauce if needed.

To serve, divide among four wide, deep bowls.

SWEET & SOUR FISH

SERVES 4

We all know sweet and sour chicken, but have you ever tried a sweet and sour whole fish on the bone? I grew up in Taiping, which has a huge Chinese population (in fact, Taiping means 'greatness in peace' in Chinese) – this is why all my family can speak Cantonese and Hokkien. It also means we had the chance to try so many different Chinese dishes. In Taiping, sweet and sour fish, which is traditionally a Cantonese dish, is served in every food court or restaurant.

This is not as sweet as a Chinese sweet and sour sauce. It's a more subtle balance of sour from the tamarind and sweetness from the sugar only, no fruit. When preparing this dish, make the sauce first so that the fish can be fried at the end to stay crisp on the outside and moist on the inside.

50g tamarind pulp

100ml cold water

1 whole sea bream (see the tip), gutted, scaled and scored (you could use sea bass, but bream is meatier)

juice of 1 lime

1 tsp fine sea salt

1 tsp light brown sugar

lots of cornflour

vegetable oil, for deep-frying

FOR THE SAUCE:

1 tbsp vegetable oil

1 tsp grated garlic

2 tbsp spice paste #3 (page 9)

100ml distilled white vinegar

2 ripe tomatoes, quartered

1 red onion, chopped

Soak the tamarind pulp in the cold water until it has dissolved. Set aside 2 tablespoons for marinating the fish and use the rest for the sauce.

To make the sauce, heat the tablespoon of oil in a wok or large frying pan on a medium-high heat. Add the garlic and cook for just 20 seconds, then add the spice paste, reduce the heat to low and cook for 2 minutes. Gradually add the tamarind juice (except for the 2 tablespoons reserved for the fish) and cook, stirring, for 1–2 minutes. Add the vinegar and increase the heat to high to let the sauce reduce slightly, but not too much or you won't have enough sauce.

Add the tomatoes, onions, pepper and 1 tablespoon of brown sugar. Cook for about 5 minutes to soften the veg. Add half of the spring onions and the salt and cook for a few minutes, until the sauce has reduced a little more. At the very end, stir in the remaining spring onions, the cucumber and the final tablespoon of sugar. Set aside and keep warm while you fry the fish.

Put the whole fish in a large bowl with the reserved tamarind juice and the lime juice, salt and brown sugar. Toss to coat the fish, then rub the marinade into the skin. **>>**

TOP TIP
If a whole fish is too big for your
pan or fryer, cut it in half or you
could even use fillets and adjust
the cooking time accordingly.

1 small white onion, chopped

1 red pepper, chopped

2 tbsp light brown sugar

2–3 spring onions, thickly chopped

1 tsp fine sea salt

½ cucumber, deseeded and chopped

TO SERVE:
boiled rice

Put plenty of cornflour in a large, shallow baking tray or baking dish. Dip the fish in the cornflour, turning it to coat it completely. Dip it back in the marinade, then coat it once more in cornflour.

Heat the oil in a large, wide, high-sided saucepan or deep-fryer to 180°C. Carefully add the fish to the hot oil and deep-fry for 10 minutes on each side, until cooked through and crisp.

Transfer the deep-fried fish to a serving platter and spoon over the sauce. Serve family-style with boiled rice for a feast.

Kway teow soup

KWAY TEOW SOUP
CHICKEN AND RICE NOODLE SOUP

SERVES 4

When I visit my hometown of Taiping, there is one market stall that I always go to. It's called Siang Malam (which means 'day and night') and is open from 10 p.m. till dawn. At the weekend the place is jam-packed with people who are catching up with friends and family. When I fly back to Malaysia and I'm in the taxi from the airport, the kway teow soup at Siang Malam is the thing I most want to seek out and eat.

2 litres chicken broth (page 11 or a well-flavoured broth or stock)

1 tbsp sesame oil, plus extra to drizzle

½ tsp oyster sauce

400g thick, flat rice noodles (10mm)

200g cooked, shredded chicken (e.g. poached chicken from the broth on page 11)

4 spring onions, cut into pieces 2–3cm long

2 fresh red chillies, thinly sliced

shop-bought fish balls, sliced (you can get these in Asian shops)

shop-bought fish cakes, sliced (you can get these in Asian shops)

a handful of fresh mustard leaves

thinly sliced pak choi

a handful of beansprouts

a handful of fresh coriander leaves

TO SEASON AT THE TABLE:

thinly sliced fresh red chilli and/or chilli oil

shop-bought crispy shallots

soy sauce

Heat the broth in a large saucepan with the sesame oil and oyster sauce. Bring up to a simmer and keep warm.

Meanwhile, cook the noodles as per the packet instructions, then drain.

To serve, divide the noodles among deep soup bowls. Add the rest of the ingredients and ladle in the broth, then add a final drizzle of sesame oil to each bowl.

Season to taste at the table with extra chillies or chilli oil, crispy shallots and soy sauce. The deeply flavoured broth will have been diluted by the starchy noodles, so you'll need to bring the flavour back up.

KWAY TEOW KUNGFU
CHARRED NOODLES WITH CHICKEN & PRAWNS

SERVES 2

When I was 12 I started working after school in a famous Chinese restaurant in Taiping called Medo that cooked all kinds of Asian and European dishes. I was only a kitchen helper butchering chickens and prepping vegetables but it's where I started to learn about the cook's life. Every night when I finished work at midnight, just before I tidied up the kitchen, I always got a phone call from my mother asking me to bring her home a takeaway of kway teow kungfu. The owner would drop me home at 12:30 and my mother would still be up, waiting for me. She was always looking forward to her kway teow kungfu and to chatting about the day.

1 tbsp vegetable oil

1 tbsp sesame oil

1 tsp grated garlic

100g boneless, skinless chicken thigh or fillet, finely chopped

1 small carrot, thinly sliced at a deep angle

1 tbsp oyster sauce

200ml broth from the chicken sambal on page 20 or the regular chicken broth on page 11

6 fresh prawns, shelled and deveined

1 egg

1 head of baby pak choi, broken into individual leaves

2 tsp slaked cornflour (i.e. cornflour mixed with a little liquid)

First cook the rice noodles according to the packet instructions. Drain and set aside.

Heat the vegetable and sesame oils in a large wok or frying pan on a medium heat. Add the garlic and cook for 30 seconds, just until fragrant. Add the chicken, increase the heat to high and stir-fry for 1–2 minutes, until lightly coloured.

Add the carrot and oyster sauce and stir-fry for 1 minute, then pour in the broth and simmer for a few minutes more. Add the prawns and cook for 2 minutes, until just cooked. Don't overcook or they'll turn rubbery.

Crack in the egg, stirring to combine, then add the pak choi leaves and the cornflour to thicken the sauce. Take the pan off the heat.

To finish, heat the vegetable and sesame oils on a high heat in a separate wok. Add the cooked, drained noodles and the ketjap manis, tossing to heat them through and colour, almost until they're charred. You want the noodles to be a bit sticky and crisp.

To serve, divide the noodles between two wide, shallow bowls. Pour over the sauce and contents of the first wok or pan, then garnish with whatever you like.

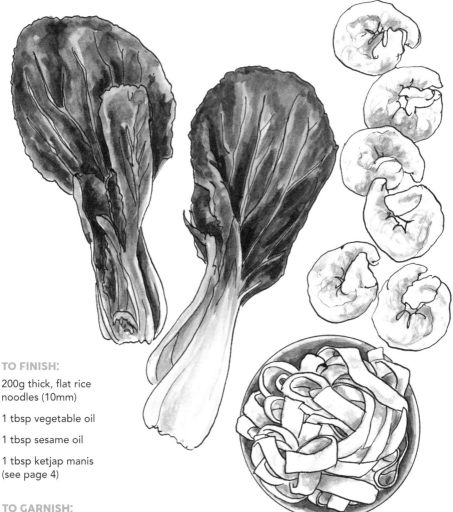

TO FINISH:

200g thick, flat rice noodles (10mm)

1 tbsp vegetable oil

1 tbsp sesame oil

1 tbsp ketjap manis (see page 4)

TO GARNISH:

a handful of beansprouts

a handful of peanuts

thinly sliced fresh red chilli

thinly sliced spring onions

a drizzle of soy sauce

lime wedges

COOK CLEVER

This recipe uses all the same garnishes as the char kway teow on the next page, so factor that into your meal planning for the week to get two different dishes from the same ingredients.

CHAR KWAY TEOW
STIR-FRIED RICE NOODLES WITH PRAWNS

SERVES 2

Char kway teow is a famous street food in Penang. Every hawker stall will serve char kway teow but the best versions are cooked on a high-heat charcoal stove with a hand fan controlling the heat to give it a good smoky, charred flavour. You can see with your own eyes how skilful the cooks at the hawker stalls are when they cook this dish of fried noodles.

This dish is similar to pad thai. Malaysia borders Thailand, so it's like pad thai travelled 100km down the road and picked up a few different twists and flavours along the way. The trick to this dish is to have everything prepped in advance and ready to go before you heat up your wok and start cooking, as this takes only minutes to make. This recipe uses all the same garnishes as the kway teow kungfu on page 48, so factor that into your meal planning for the week.

200g thick, flat rice noodles (10mm)

1 tbsp vegetable oil

1 tsp grated garlic

1 tbsp spice paste #3 (page 9)

16 fresh prawns, shelled and deveined

2 tbsp dark soy sauce

1 tsp oyster sauce

2 spring onions, thinly sliced at an angle

3–4 tbsp chicken broth (page 11 or a well-flavoured broth or stock)

1 egg

a drizzle of sesame oil

TO GARNISH:

a handful of beansprouts

a handful of peanuts

thinly sliced fresh red chilli

thinly sliced spring onions

a drizzle of soy sauce

lime wedges

Cook the noodles according to the packet instructions, then drain.

Heat the vegetable oil in a large wok or frying pan on a medium heat. Add the garlic and cook for 30 seconds, until fragrant. Add the spice paste and cook for 30 seconds, then add the prawns, dark soy sauce and oyster sauce and stir-fry for 1 minute.

Add the cooked, drained noodles, the spring onions and the chicken broth. Turn up the heat to high and continue to cook, stirring constantly, to reduce the sauce.

Crack in the egg and cook for 1 minute, stirring to bring it all together, then add a drizzle of sesame oil.

Divide the noodles between two plates and garnish with whatever you'd like. Eat straight away because the noodles get too soft and stodgy if they go cold.

TAUHU SUMBAT
MALAYSIAN STUFFED TOFU

MAKES 12

Tauhu sumbat is another street food you'll see everywhere in Malaysia and is particularly popular during Ramadan. It's the perfect way to serve tofu, which is bland if you don't do anything with it. But deep-frying gives it a crisp, crunchy texture. Then when you dip it into the nutty satay sauce, the tofu will soak it up, making you go for a second dip. Try to get a big block of tofu in an Asian market, as you want big chunky squares for this, but really the satay sauce is the star.

1kg Chinese soft tofu or silken tofu (see the intro)

vegetable oil, for frying

1 carrot, grated or julienned

1 cucumber, grated or julienned

a handful of beansprouts

satay sauce (page 10), warmed, to serve

Cut the tofu into 6 x 3cm cubes. Pat dry.

Heat the oil in a high-sided pan on a high heat – you need enough oil to come halfway up the sides of the tofu. Add the tofu cubes and shallow-fry for a few minutes on each side, until light golden brown. (Alternatively, you could deep-fry the cubes in a deep-fryer at 190°C for 5 minutes.) You want a golden-brown crust all over but the inside should still be creamy and white. Transfer to a plate or chopping board and allow to rest for a few minutes to firm up. (Frying the tofu improves the texture, but it isn't strictly necessary. You could just heat through the plain tofu in the sauce if you want to skip this step.)

Cut each cube in half on the diagonal to make two triangles. Cut a slit into the creamy white centre and squeeze the sides of the cube to open it up slightly to make a pocket. Stuff with the carrots, cucumbers and beansprouts.

Put the stuffed tofu on a plate and spoon around plenty of warm satay sauce. Or serve it deconstructed, with the veg on the side of the fried tofu.

GAENG PRIK KHIAO WAAN
THAI GREEN CURRY

SERVES 4

I always say that whatever I put into a dish, I want to get it back – I want to taste all the ingredients, so everything should be there for a reason. For me, this is the perfect way to eat aubergine, green beans and tofu. You can use any veg you like but cook hard veg like carrots or squash longer than soft veg like broccoli, green beans and aubergine. It's comforting to eat when you've had enough meat for the week.

1 block of tofu, cubed

2 tbsp vegetable oil, plus extra for deep-frying

1 shallot, chopped

1 tsp grated garlic

2–3 lime leaves, torn (see page 4)

4 tbsp green spice paste (page 9)

juice of 1 lime

1 tbsp caster sugar

1 tbsp fish sauce

1 tsp fine sea salt

1 x 400ml tin of full-fat coconut milk

2 tbsp soy sauce

1 carrot, chopped

½ small squash, chopped

a handful of broccoli florets

a handful of green beans, chopped

½ aubergine, chopped

Deep-fry the tofu until it's golden brown all over. Drain on kitchen paper and set aside.

Heat 1 tablespoon of the oil in a large saucepan on a medium heat. Add the shallot, garlic and lime leaves and cook for 2 minutes, until fragrant. Add the spice paste and the other tablespoon of oil and cook for 2 minutes, stirring constantly.

Add the lime juice, sugar, fish sauce and salt and cook for 30 seconds, then stir in the coconut milk and soy sauce. Turn the heat up to high and add the carrot and squash (or any hard veg you're using). Bring to a boil, then reduce the heat to a simmer for 8–10 minutes, stirring occasionally, until reduced slightly.

Add the broccoli, green beans and aubergine (or any soft veg you're using). Simmer for 5 minutes, then add the tofu to heat it through. Keep cooking until the sauce is nice and thick – it should be coating the veg, which should all still be holding their shape. When my mother cooks this dish she will reduce the sauce a little bit more than usual to allow all the flavour from the green curry to bind nicely with the vegetables.

Finish with the shredded lime leaf, lime juice and a final teaspoon each of sugar and fish sauce. I serve this with jasmine rice because it has more starch and is a little stickier than other kinds of rice, so it works beautifully to soak up the curry sauce.

TO FINISH:

1 lime leaf, shredded

juice of ½ lime

1 tsp caster sugar

1 tsp fish sauce

TO SERVE:

boiled jasmine rice

BAO TWO WAYS

MAKES 12

I went to St George's School in Taiping, where fresh-cooked food was served in the school canteen. Bao pao – a steamed bun with your filling of choice – was one of the options. When I was a kid we just bought them and ate them without any big fuss. Years later, when I went back to Malaysia for my sister's wedding in 2014, we decided to go on a road trip. In Malaysia there is always a rest stop every 30–50 miles with a different food truck at each one. At one of them a food truck was serving steamed buns that were colour coded with a dot of food colouring for the different fillings: yellow for curry chicken, green for tuna, red for sweet red bean paste or plain for a kaya (coconut custard) filling. We bought half a dozen mixed baos.

When I came back to Ireland and heard about the new bao trend in every corner of Dublin, I was fascinated by it. I grew up with bao but never thought much of it until I saw all the different ways of serving it. I started making them and serving them in my restaurant. Then I shared this recipe with my great chef friend Kevin O'Toole, who was the chef at the Chameleon restaurant in Temple Bar at the time. He didn't take long to master this homemade bao recipe and went on to create many different flavours that got great reviews from the food critics.

Try filling bao with leftover rendang or curry, but the key is that the filling must be cold and dry. But having said that, concentrate on the bao rather than the filling. Getting the bao itself right is more important.

175ml warm water

1 x 7g sachet of fast-acting dried yeast or 50g fresh yeast

175ml milk

1 egg

500–600g bapao wheat flour (see the tip)

1 tsp fine sea salt

1 tsp caster sugar

FOR THE FILLING:

leftover lamb rendang (page 34), curry (page 26) or anything you like, really

Pour the warm water into a large jug and sprinkle over the yeast. Set aside for 10 minutes to allow the yeast to activate – it will get nice and frothy – then whisk in the milk and egg.

Put 500g of the flour in a large bowl with the salt and sugar and whisk together. Pour in the wet ingredients and mix to combine. It will be very wet so mix in another 50g of flour, then knead until smooth, supple and elastic. It should be nice and soft.

Put the dough in a bowl, cover it with cling film and allow to prove in a warm, draught-free place until doubled in size. This could take anywhere from 45 minutes to 2 hours depending on how warm your kitchen is.

Line each of the three bases of a steamer with a piece of non-stick baking paper. >>

Dust the countertop with the remaining bapao flour and tip out the dough. Don't knock it back – the dough is quite soft and fragile, so knead it gently.

To make stuffed bao, divide the dough into 12 balls. Working with one ball at a time, flatten it into a disc. Put ½ tablespoon of your cold, dry filling in the middle, then enclose it by pinching the dough up around it (see the freezer tip). Put the ball in the lined steamer, then repeat with the rest of the dough and filling. Put four balls on each tier of the steamer, spaced well apart. Cover the steamer and allow the dough to prove again for about 1 hour, until the balls have doubled in size. Note that the greasier your filling is, the longer it will take the dough to rise.

To make unfilled bao buns (what I call Pac-Man buns), cut out 12 small rectangular strips of non-stick baking paper and set them aside. Divide the dough into 12 balls. Using a rolling pin, roll out each ball into a disc. Put a strip of paper on the bottom half of each disc, then fold over the other half on top of the paper so that it looks like a taco. The strip of paper will prevent the dough from sticking together as it proves and cooks (see the freezer tip). Put four bao buns on each tier of the steamer, spaced well apart. Cover the steamer and allow the dough to prove again for about 1 hour, until doubled in size.

No matter which type of bao you've made, set the steamer over a pan of simmering water. Cook for 25–30 minutes, until the dough is light and bouncy. Serve the stuffed bao while warm or use the Pac-Man buns for whatever filling you like.

ROTI CANAI

MAKES 8

Roti brings out the mamak (Indian-Malay-Chinese) side of me! There's no cutlery needed with roti – just wash your hands and you're ready to go. Roti is a thin, crispy bread cooked in a large, flat cast iron pan until it's nearly burnt to give it a nice toasted flavour. It's often served with dal, sambal or pickled onion. It's the same recipe that you use to make the chicken murtabak on page 24, which is commonly eaten at mamak stalls all over Malaysia for breakfast. You can also pick your choice of curry to serve with it during lunchtime; we sometimes eat it with chicken curry and sambal. When you go for a night out in Ireland you always end up in a chipper but in Malaysia we always end up at a mamak stall for roti and teh tarik (page 64) before we make our way home.

500g plain flour

1 tsp fine sea salt

1 tsp caster sugar

200ml condensed milk

100ml water

2 eggs, beaten

50g very soft salted butter, plus extra for cooking

vegetable oil, for cooking and greasing

Put the flour, salt and sugar in a large bowl and whisk to combine. I always reserve a bit of this flour mixture to dust the countertop with – this way, the proportions of the ingredients stay correct.

Whisk together the condensed milk, water and eggs in a separate small bowl, then add the wet to the dry ingredients. Knead until it comes together into a smooth, supple dough.

Put the dough in a large bowl, cover with cling film and put it in a warm place to relax for 30 minutes.

Lightly dust the countertop with the reserved flour mixture. Tip the dough out onto the countertop and roll it into a log, then divide it into eight even portions.

Use some of the soft butter to grease a large mixing bowl. Shape each portion into a ball, then brush it liberally with the soft butter. Put the balls in the bowl, nestled together and touching. Cover the bowl with cling film and put it in the fridge overnight.

The next day, take the bowl out of the fridge and allow the dough to come back to room temperature. Lightly oil your countertop. Usually you need flour to roll out a dough, but for roti, you need to use oil – and the more oil you use, the easier it will be to stretch out the dough. **>>**

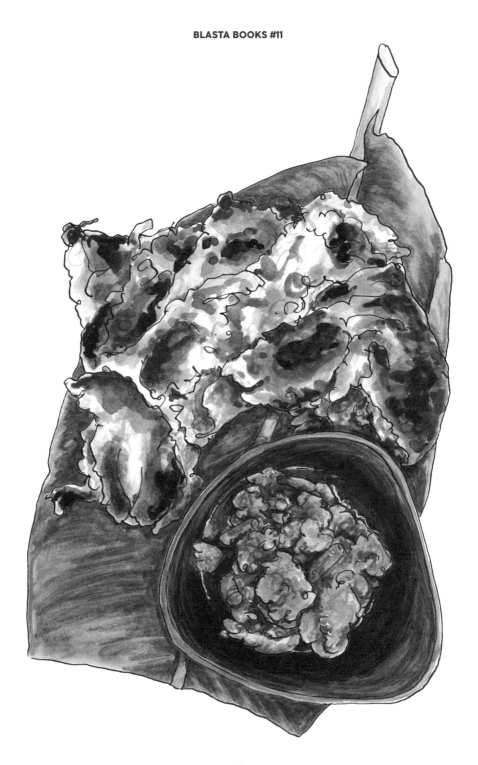

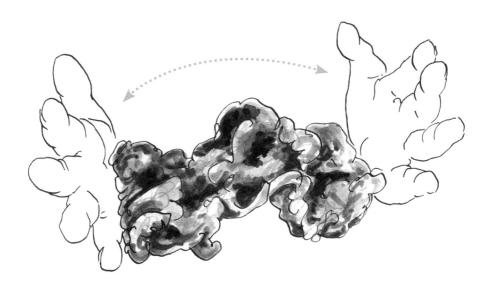

Working with one ball of dough at a time, put it on the countertop and press it out flat with your fingertips, then pull and stretch it out to make it as thin and transparent as possible. Lift it off the countertop every 10 seconds so that it doesn't stick. It will be an irregular shape and holes might form around the edges as you stretch the dough, but that's okay. Once it's thin enough, fold in the edges to make it into a square.

Heat 1 tablespoon of oil in a large non-stick pan on a high heat until it's piping hot. Put the square roti in the pan and cook for 1–2 minutes, until golden brown, almost like a crêpe. Flip it over and cook for 1–2 minutes more.

Add a knob of butter to the pan and let it melt over the roti, then slide the roti out onto a chopping board. Put your hands on either side of the warm roti, then clap your hands together, smashing the roti in between your hands to scrunch it up a bit. Repeat with the rest of the dough.

Serve warm with sambal oelek or dal.

COOK CLEVER
This roti is an essential part of the chicken murtabak on page 24.

SOM TAM
MANGO AND PAPAYA SLAW

SERVES 4

When we were kids, my mother used to bring us to visit our family on the Malaysian border of Thailand during Wesak Day (Buddha Day) or Songkran (Thai New Year). We'd always have som tam with our dinner, using the unripe mango and papaya from the garden.

1 green (unripe) papaya or Granny Smith apple, peeled and cut into matchsticks

1 large, ripe mango, peeled and cut into matchsticks

1 cucumber, cut into matchsticks

10 raw green beans, chopped

2 fresh red chillies, cut into matchsticks

a handful of fresh coriander, chopped

1 lime leaf, shredded

40g dry roasted peanuts, chopped

juice of 3 limes

2–3 tbsp fish sauce

1–2 tbsp light brown sugar

1 tsp grated garlic

1 head of Baby Gem lettuce, broken into individual leaves, to serve (optional)

Put all the ingredients except the Baby Gem (if using) in a large bowl with 2 tablespoons of the fish sauce and 1 tablespoon of the sugar. Toss everything together with your hands, then taste and add more fish sauce and/or sugar if needed.

Line a serving bowl with the Baby Gem leaves (if using), then pile the slaw into the middle. That's it! This is best eaten straight away, when it's fresh. If you want to get ahead, prep all the ingredients but mix them together just before serving.

TRY THIS

- Scatter over some crispy bacon.
- Add black pepper chicken (page 22) to make this into a substantial salad.
- Add cooked glass noodles, chopped bird's eye chilli and a little extra fish sauce and sugar to make this into a noodle dish.
- Add cooked glass noodles and roll it all up in a rice paper wrapper to make a summer roll.

ACAR BEREMPAH
SPICED VEG PICKLE

SERVES 4–6

This dish of half-cooked spiced pickled vegetables is served at weddings and food stalls all over Malaysia.

1 tbsp vegetable oil

3 garlic cloves, quartered

1 tsp black mustard seeds

1 tbsp spice paste #5 (page 9)

1 tsp Baba's Meat Curry Powder (see the note on page 25)

¼ tsp ground turmeric

1 carrot, thinly sliced

1 small red onion, finely diced

1 small white onion, finely diced

100ml distilled white vinegar

1 fresh red chilli, thinly sliced

1 tbsp sesame seeds

2 tsp caster sugar

1 tsp fine sea salt

1 cucumber, halved lengthways, deseeded and thinly sliced

1 tbsp light brown sugar

Heat the oil in a large saucepan on a medium heat. Add the garlic and mustard seeds and cook for about 1 minute, until the garlic is fragrant and the mustard seeds start to pop. Add the spice paste and cook for 30 seconds, then add the curry powder and turmeric and cook for 30 seconds more.

Add the carrot, onions and vinegar and let it bubble up, then add the chilli, sesame seeds and 1 teaspoon of the caster sugar. Increase the heat to high and let it bubble up again for 1–2 minutes, then add the salt and another teaspoon of caster sugar. Reduce the heat to medium-high and simmer until the vinegar has reduced but not completely evaporated.

Use a slotted spoon to transfer the veg to a serving bowl so they keep their crunch and stir in the sliced cucumber. Put the pan back on the heat, add the brown sugar and cook until the vinegar has reduced until it's thick and syrupy. Pour it over the veg in the bowl and allow to cool.

Serve the pickle cold or at room temperature on the side of just about anything. This will keep for a few days in the fridge.

HOT MILO
MALAYSIAN HOT CHOCOLATE

SERVES 2

If you drink Milo, it will make you big and strong or you will become a professional athlete. Well, that's what I thought anyway when I drank Milo as a kid since the branding always shows a picture of an athlete. On sports day in school, there would be a Milo van in the corner serving small cups of hot or cold Milo. We would each get two coupons to be redeemed for the Milo. After all these years, I still drink it. I always buy it whenever I see it in an Asian market and now my kids drink Milo too.

6 tbsp Milo powder

3 tbsp condensed milk

500ml just-boiled water

Whisk the Milo and condensed milk together in a heatproof jug (I use condensed milk to give it extra sweetness and richness). Pour in the just-boiled water and whisk to combine.

You can serve it now, as is, but traditionally the hot Milo is 'pulled' between two pitchers to froth it up. To do this, put the hot Milo in one pitcher, then pour it from a height into the second pitcher. Now pour it from that pitcher back into the first pitcher, again from a height. Keep doing this, pouring back and forth between the pitchers, until it has frothed up slightly. Alternatively, you could use a hand-held milk frother or the steamer on an espresso machine.

MILO AIS
Milo ais (Malaysian chocolate milk) is the same as hot Milo but we drink it during the daytime when the weather is a bit warm in Malaysia. To make Milo ais, just pour the hot Milo over a tall glass of ice.

TEH TARIK
MALAYSIAN PULLED TEA

SERVES 2

You will hear 'Teh tarik satu!' being called out every time you go to mamak stalls all over Malaysia. It's a hot milky tea made with condensed milk but the best part is when you see the guys in the coffee-making corner start to froth (pull) the tea from one stainless steel jug to another. They will do this a few times until the tea is frothy, then pour it into a mug to be served. It's a skill and also a bit of theatre for the customers.

2 black tea bags	Steep the tea in the just-boiled water for at least 5 minutes – you want this to be a strong brew.
500ml just-boiled water	
2–3 tbsp condensed milk	Stir in the condensed milk, then 'pull' the tea between two pitchers, as for the hot Milo on page 63, to froth it up.

CHAI

SERVES 1

This might not be the chai that you are used to getting in coffee shops because we don't use chai syrup in mamak stalls. Proper chai is made simply by simmering a handful of spices in hot water to release their flavour, then steeping the tea in this flavoured water and sweetening it to taste with condensed milk. When it's raining outside and you're sitting in a mamak stall, sitting back and drinking your chai, it's pure comfort.

500ml water	Pour the water into a small saucepan and add all the spices. Simmer for 10 minutes to extract all their flavour, then bring to a boil. Take the pan off the heat and steep your tea in the just-boiled water for 5 minutes.
4 cardamom pods	
3–4 whole black peppercorns	
2–3 cloves	
1 cinnamon stick	Discard the tea bag. Add the condensed milk and 'pull' the chai between two pitchers, as for the hot Milo on page 63, to froth it up.
1 star anise	
1 black tea bag	
1 tbsp condensed milk	

INDEX

Nine Bean Rows
23 Mountjoy Square
Dublin, D01 E0F8
Ireland
@9beanrowsbooks
ninebeanrowsbooks.com

NINE
BEAN
ROWS

Blasta Books is an imprint of Nine Bean Rows Books Ltd.
@blastabooks blastabooks.com

First published 2024
Text copyright © Sham Hanifa, 2024
Illustrations copyright © Nicky Hooper, 2024

ISBN: 978-1-7392105-5-7

Editor: Kristin Jensen

Series artist: Nicky Hooper
nickyhooper.com

Designer: Jane Matthews
janematthewsdesign.com

Proofreader: Jocelyn Doyle

Printed by L&C Printing Group, Poland

The paper in this book is produced using pulp from managed forests.

10 9 8 7 6 5 4 3 2 1

About the author

Shamzuri (Sham) Hanifa is an award-winning chef, businessman and broadcaster. Originally from Malaysia, Sham moved to Carrick-on-Shannon in County Leitrim, Ireland, in 2000 to begin a journey that would take him from general kitchen work to head chef and owner/co-owner of a number of establishments, including the Cottage Restaurant, My Kitchen by Sham Hanifa, Synergy Café, Buffalo Boy Steakhouse and the Chef Sham Sauces range.

Sham has appeared regularly on Virgin Media's *Six O'Clock Show* since 2019, where he demonstrates easy, Asian-style dishes. He is a proud member of Euro-Toques and is a Food Ambassador for County Leitrim. Married to Dympna, a local schoolteacher, and blessed with two children, Kaelan and Kayanna, his family is the motivation and driving force behind Sham and his career.

 sham__hanifa